Baroque—Classical—Romantic—Cont

Piano Literature Volu

CONTENTS

ISBN 0-8497-6009-7

Neil A. Kjos Music Company, *Publisher*

Musette in D

Bach

From the "Anna Magdalena
Bach Notebook," BWV Anh. 126

13
17
21
f
25

Minuet in d Minor

Bach

From the "Anna Magdalena Bach Notebook," BWV Anh. 132

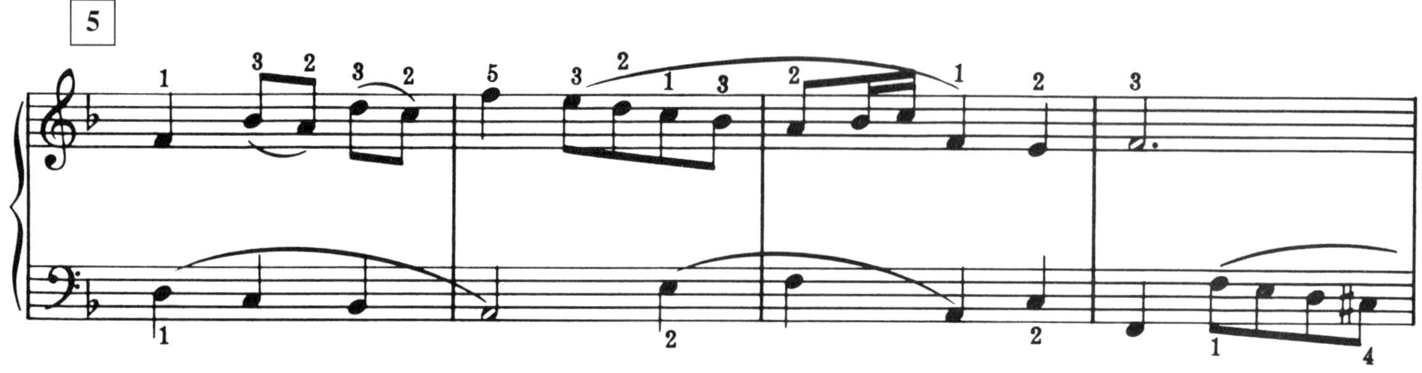

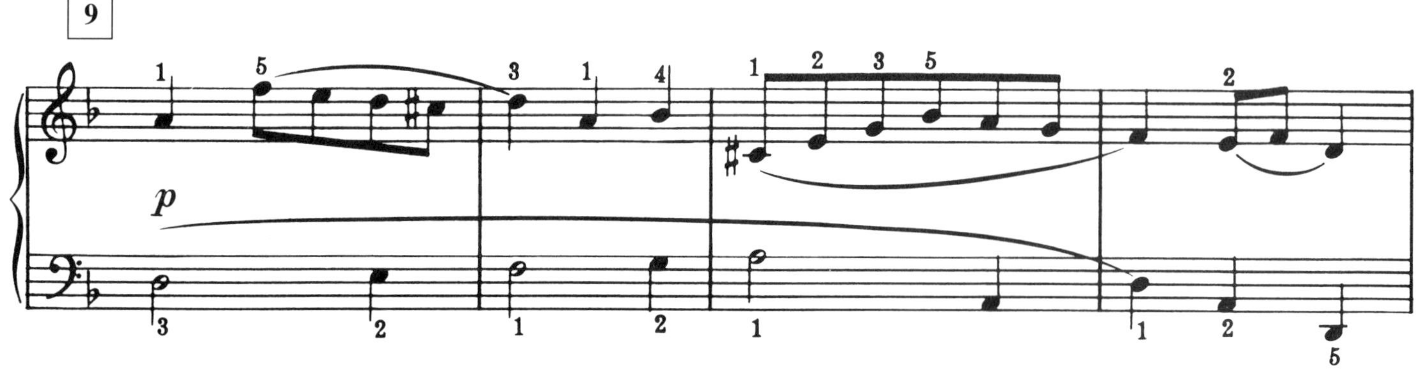

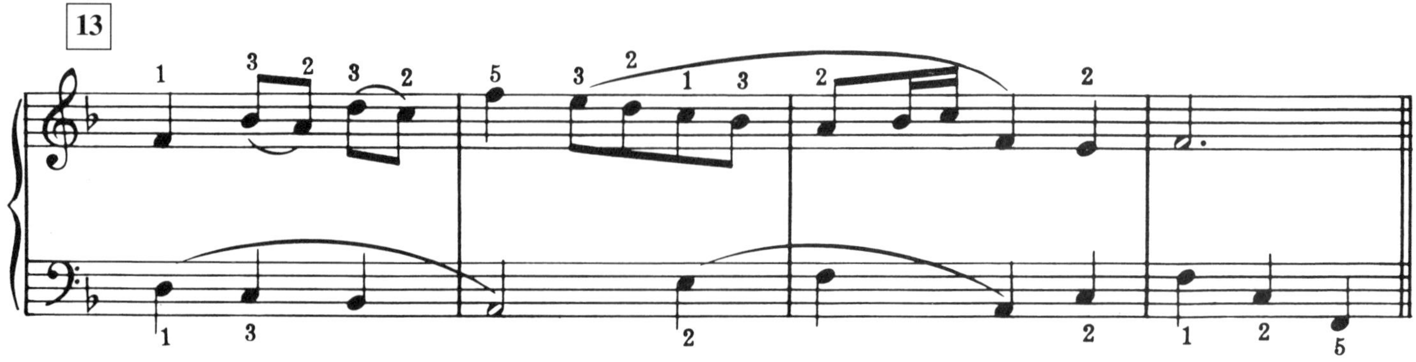

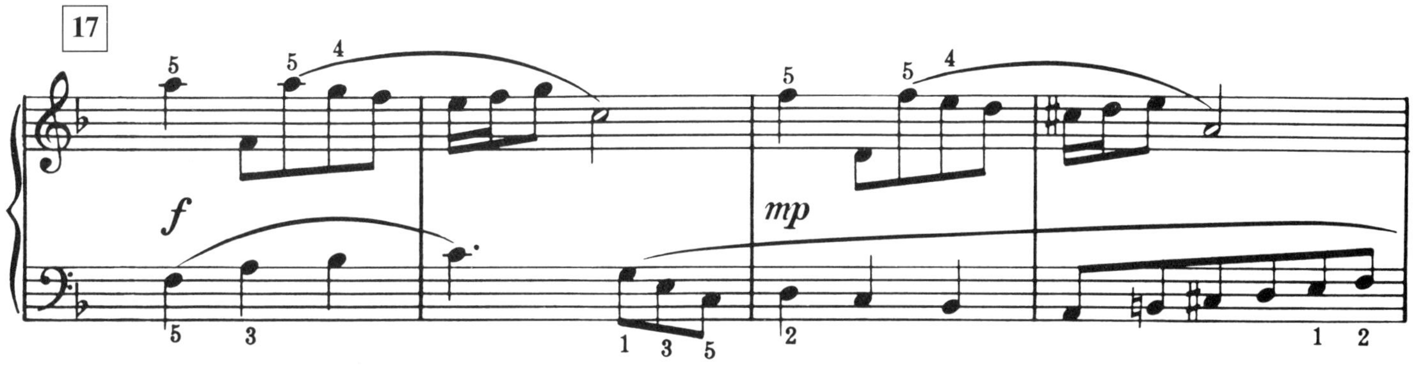
17
f
mp

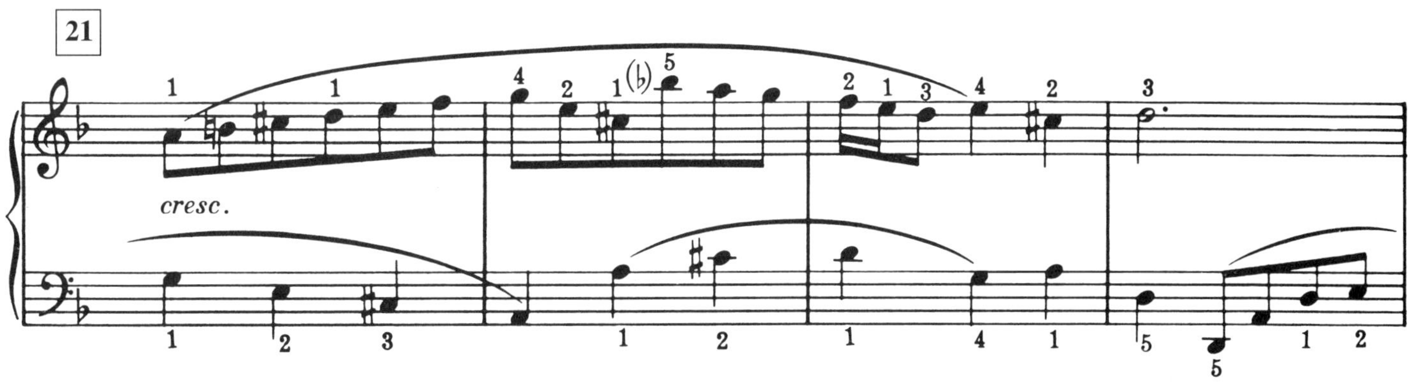
21
cresc.

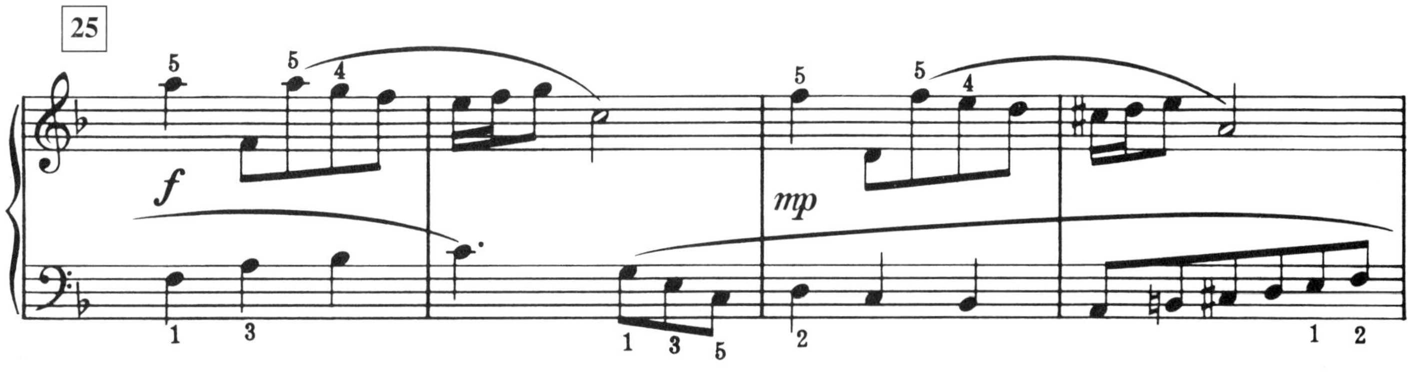
25
f
mp

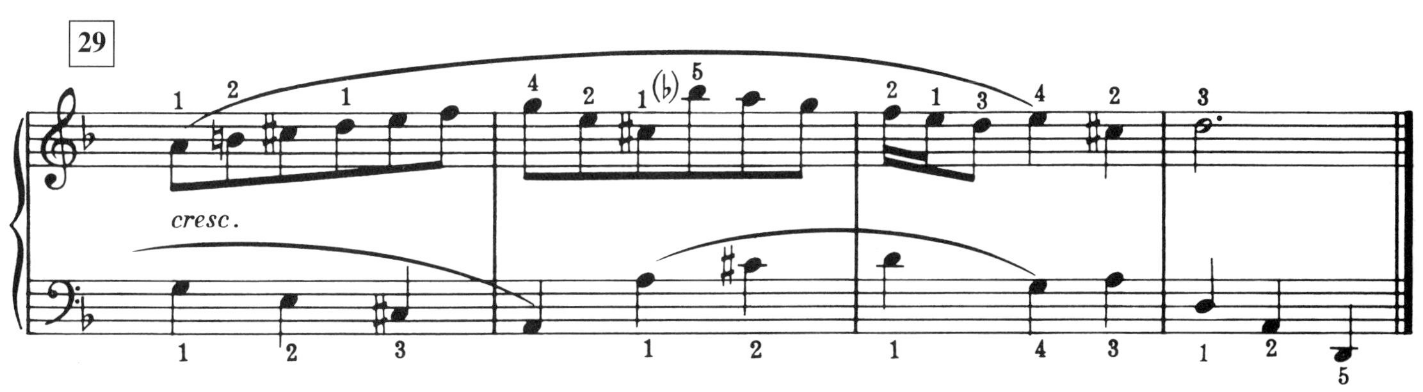
29
cresc.

Polonaise in g Minor

Bach

From the "Anna Magdalena Bach Notebook," BWV Anh. 125

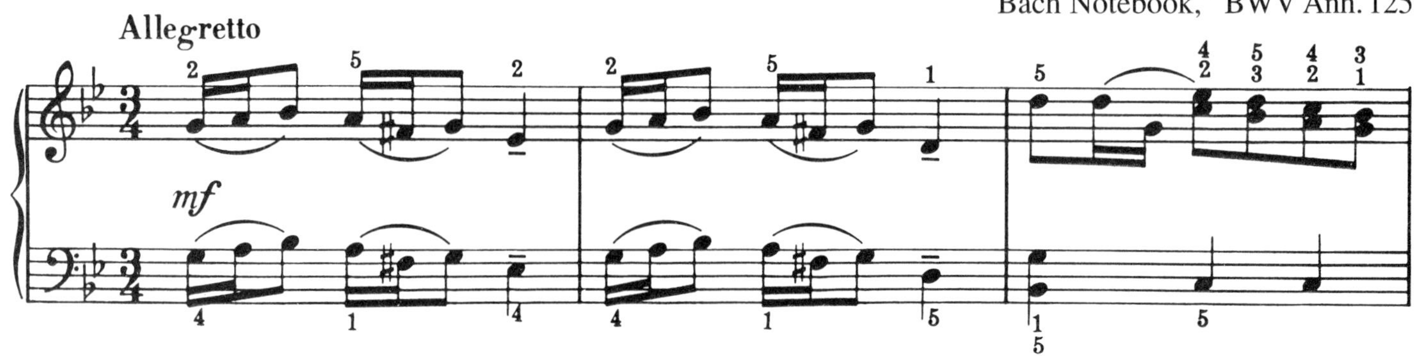

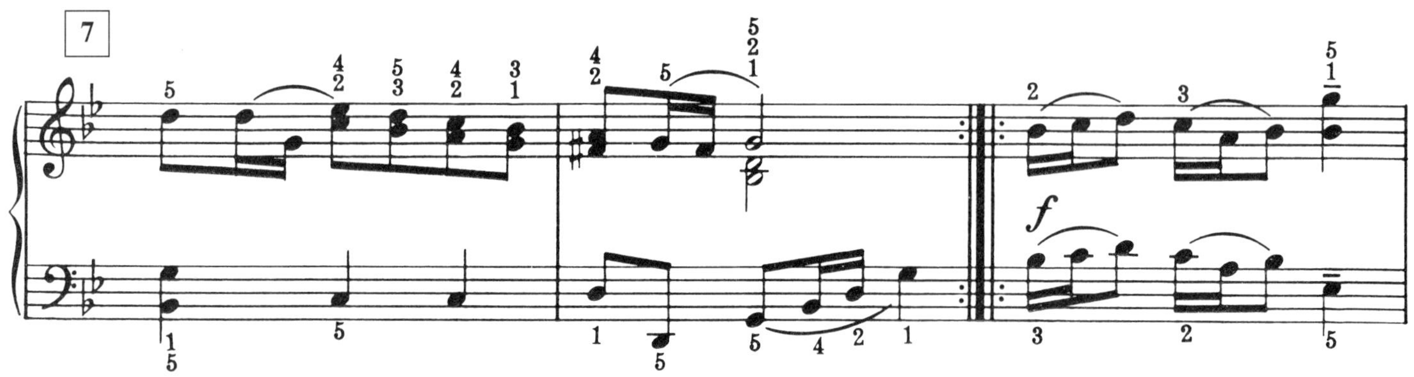

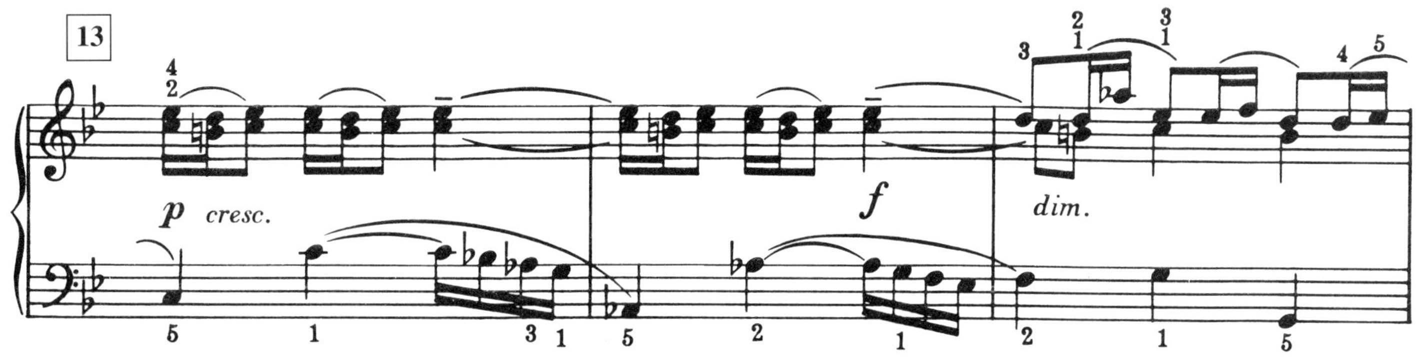
13
p cresc.
f
dim.

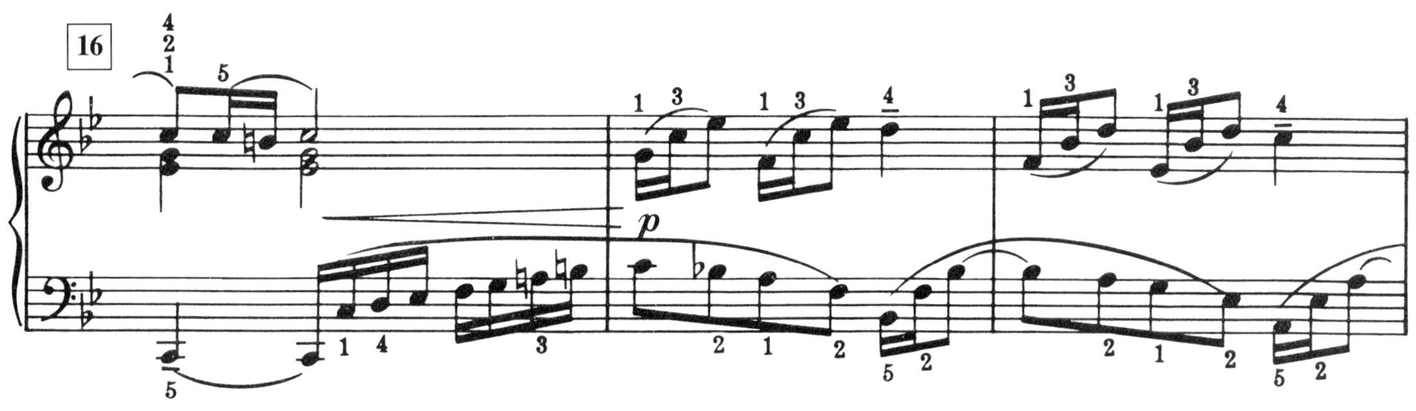
16
p

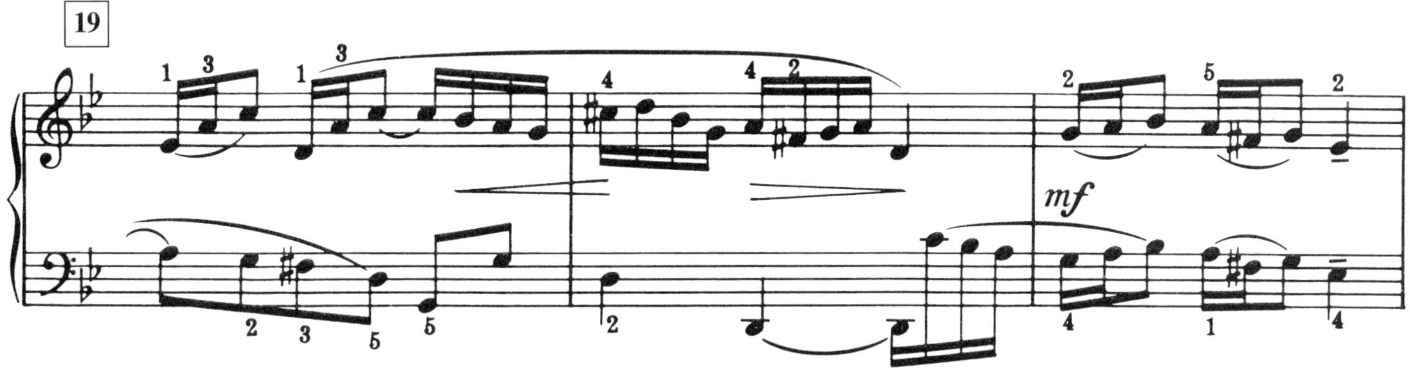
19
mf

22

Polonaise in g Minor

Bach

From the "Anna Magdalena Bach Notebook," BWV Anh. 119

Moderato

Sonatina

Clementi

Op.36, No. 1

16
p
f
21
p
26
cresc.
31
f
35

Andante
mp dolce
tr
cresc.
sfz
p
f
cresc.
sfz
p
sfz
p
mp dolce
tr
cresc.
f
tr
5
9
14
18
22

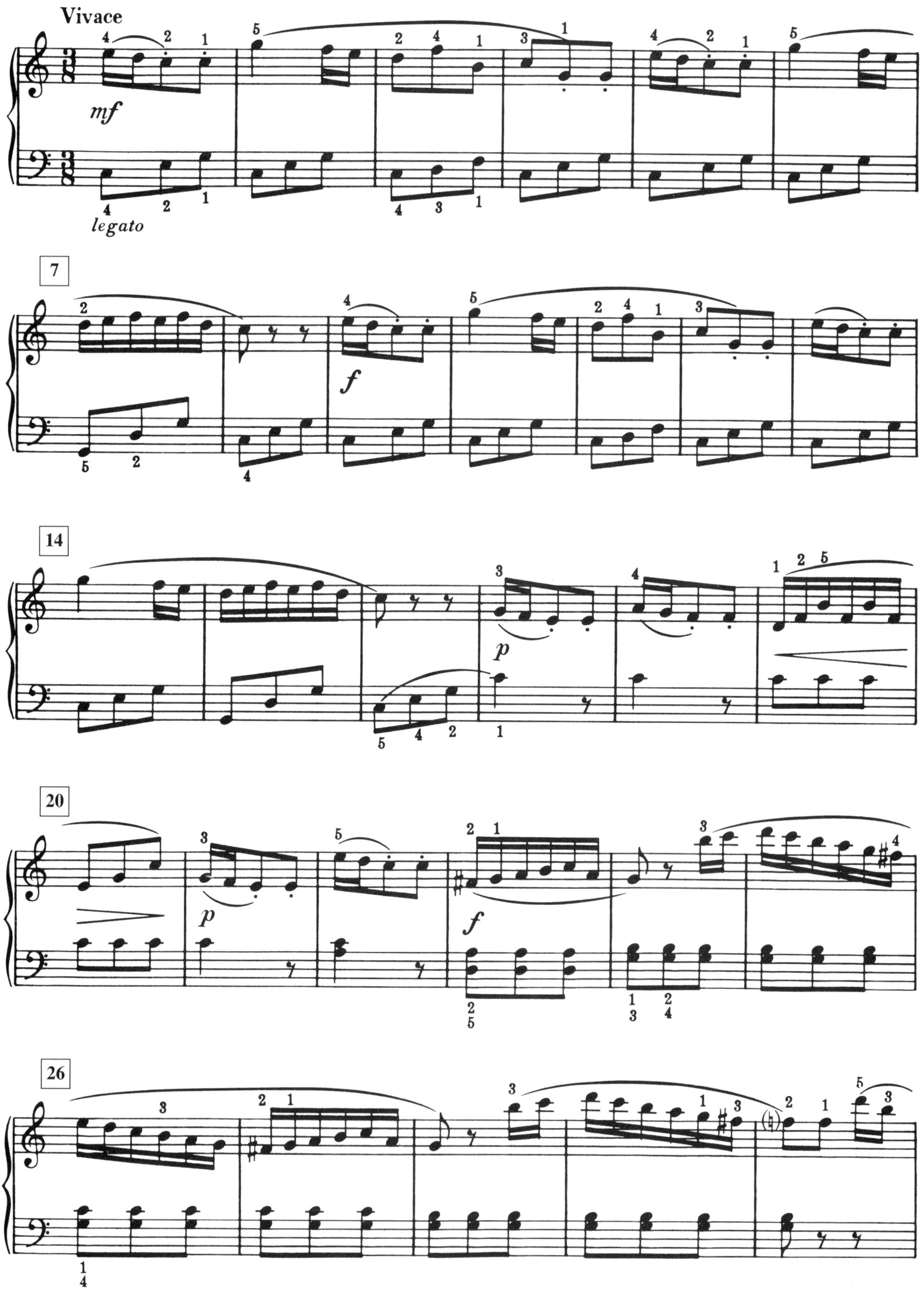
Vivace
mf
legato
7
f
14
p
20
p
f
26

31
dim.
mf
38
f
44
50
p
56
p
cresc.
63
ff

Sonatina in F

Beethoven

Anh. 5, No. 2

32
40
mp
legato
47
dim.
mp
mf
53
f
ff
58
dolce
65
cresc.
f

Rondo
Allegro
p
f
9
p
f
17
f
24
dim.
29
p
f
37
p
mf
mp
legato

45
mf
dim.
mf
mp
53
mf
mp
dim.
p
61
cresc.
69
ad lib.
dim.
a tempo
p
78
f
p
86
f
p
f

Hunting Song

Schumann

From the "Album for the Young"

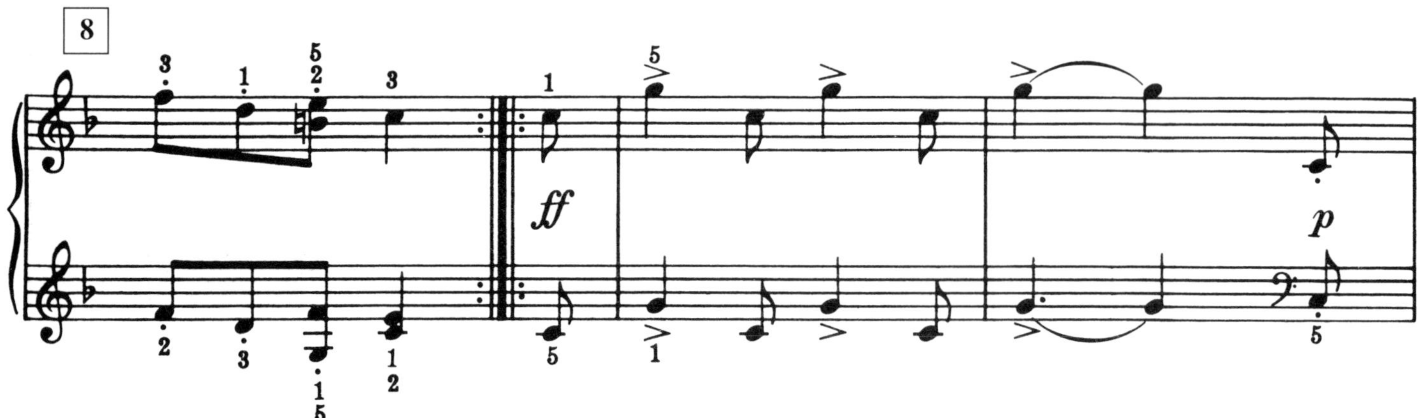

15
18
21
25
f

First Loss

Schumann

From the "Album for the Young"

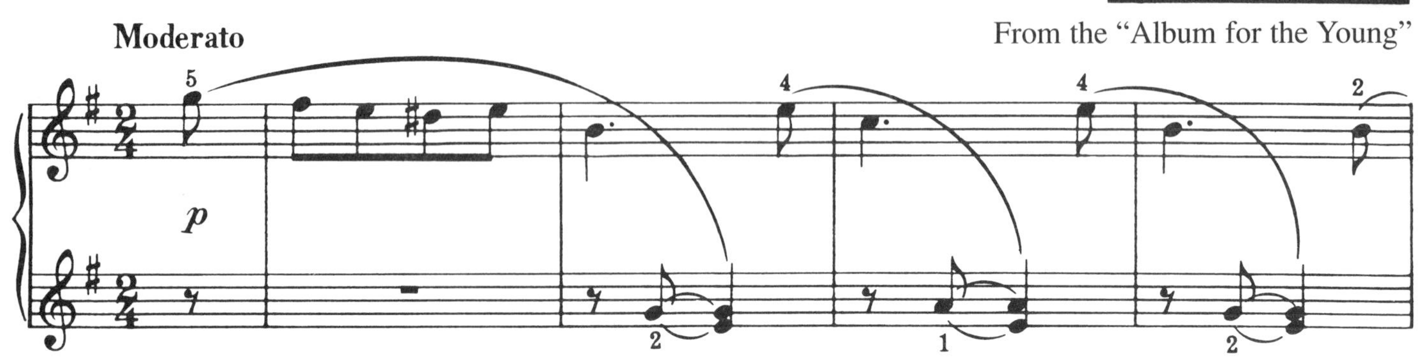

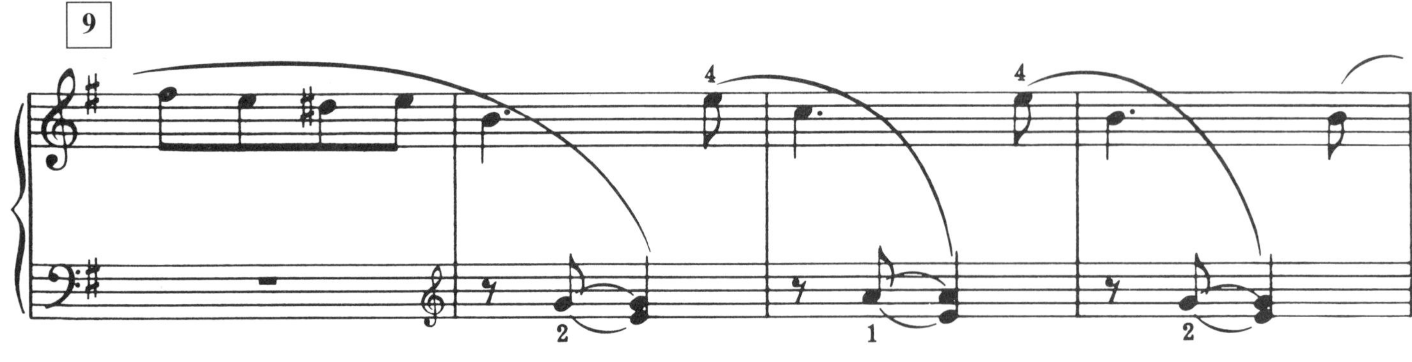

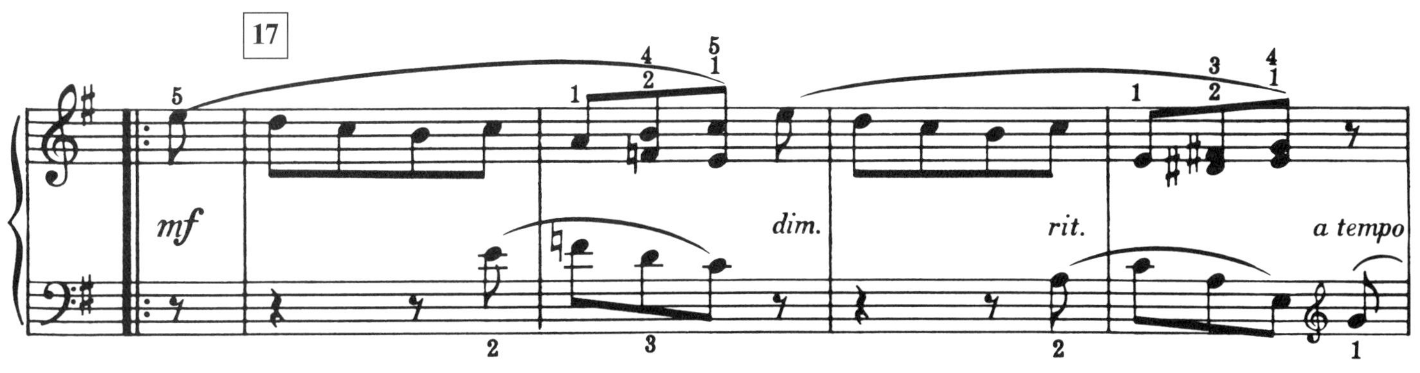
17
mf
dim.
rit.
a tempo

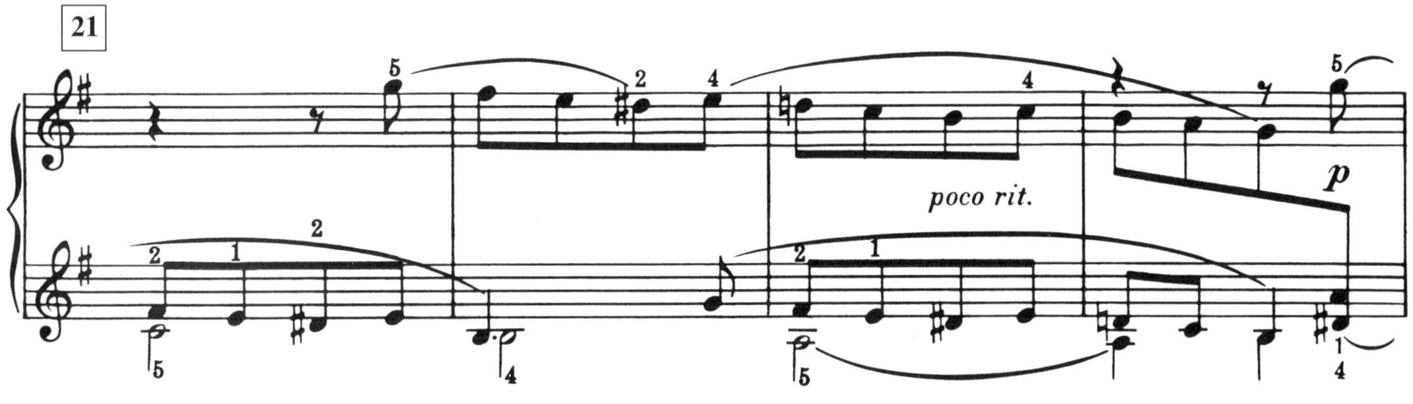
21
poco rit.
p

25
a tempo
f

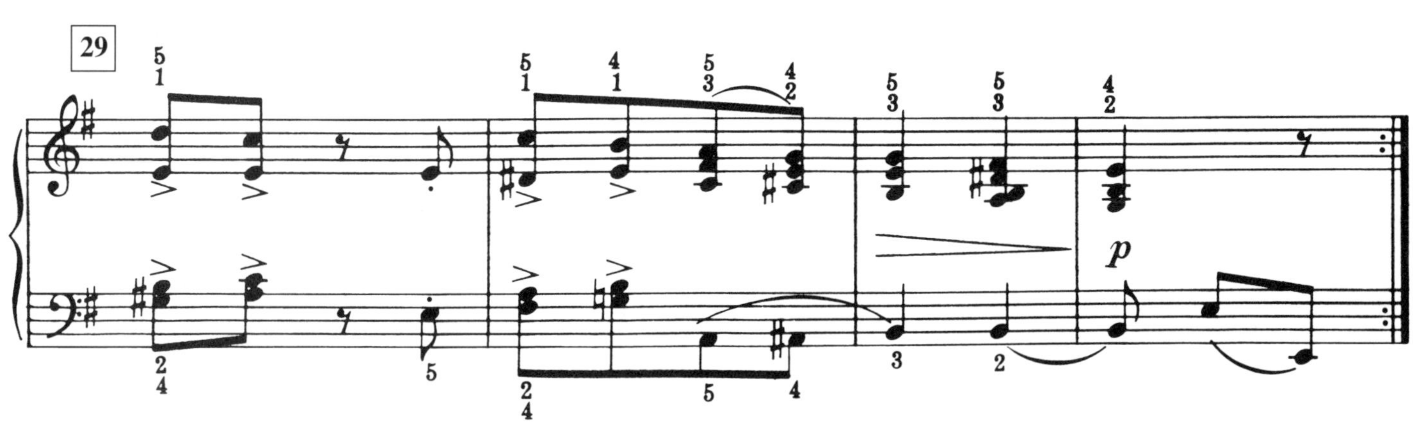
29
p

The Clown

Kabalevsky

Op. 39, No. 20

13
3
1
1
1
2
5
1
2
5

16
1
4
3
1
2
3
1
f
f
1
2
5
3
1
5

19
3
2
f

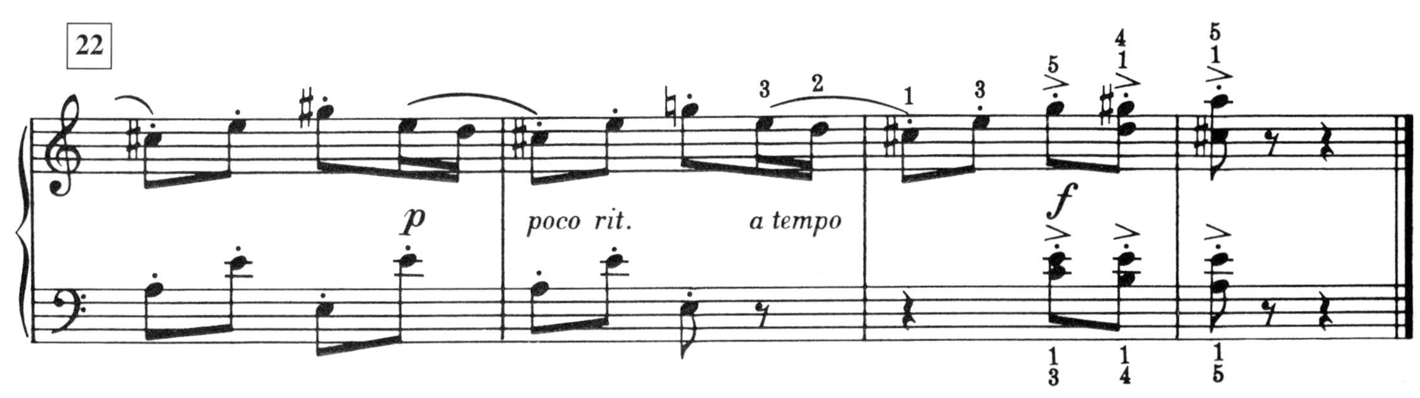
22
3
2
1
3
5
4
1
5
1
p
poco rit.
a tempo
f
1
3
1
4
1
5

Variations on a Russian Folksong

Kabalevsky

Op. 51, No. 1

Allegro

Theme

f

mp

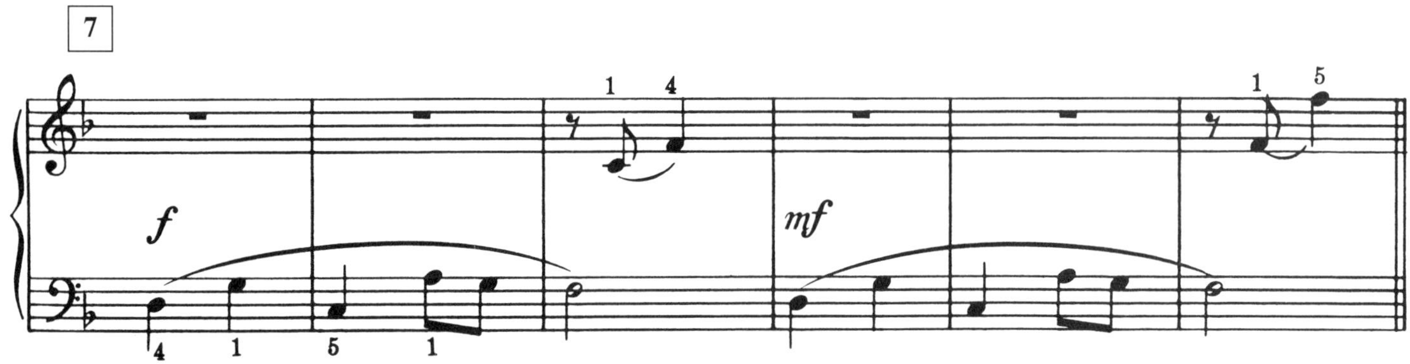

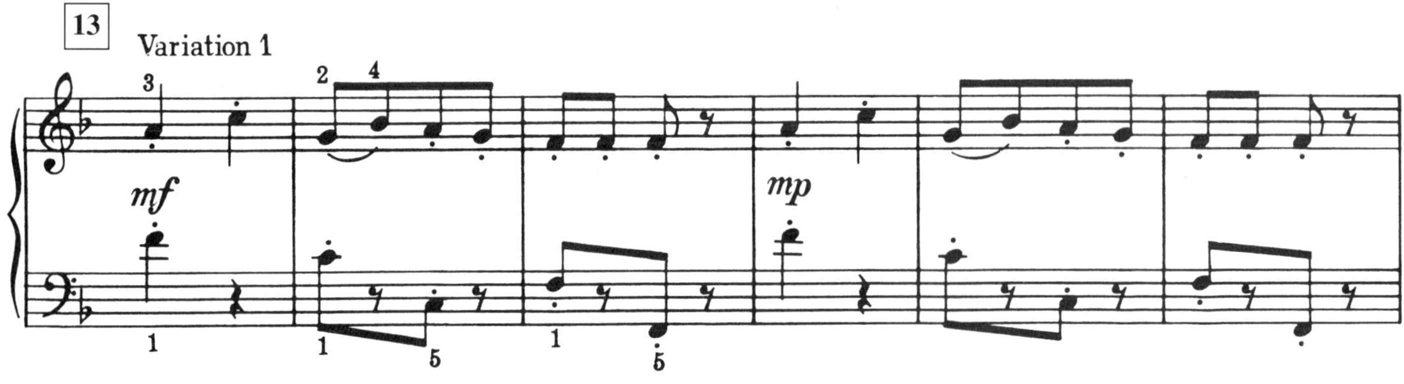

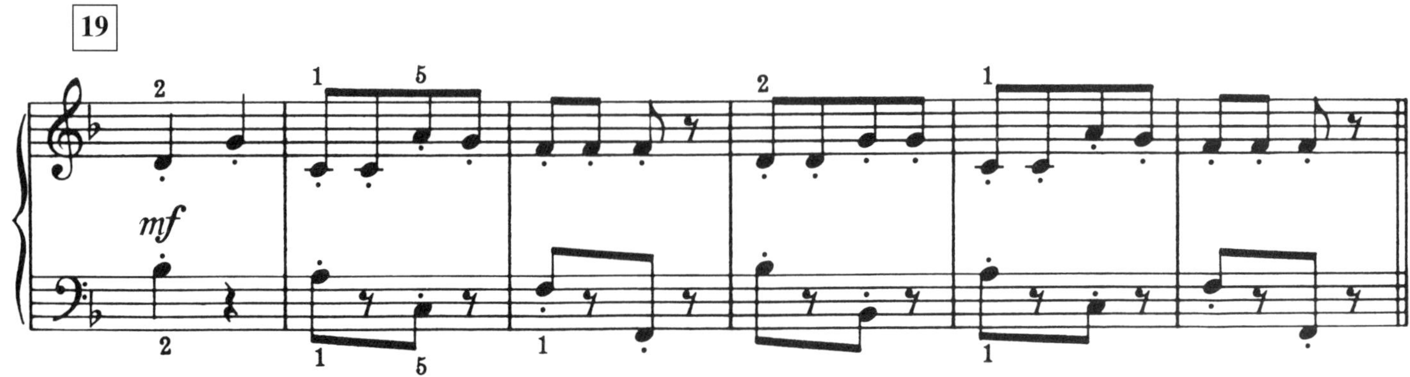

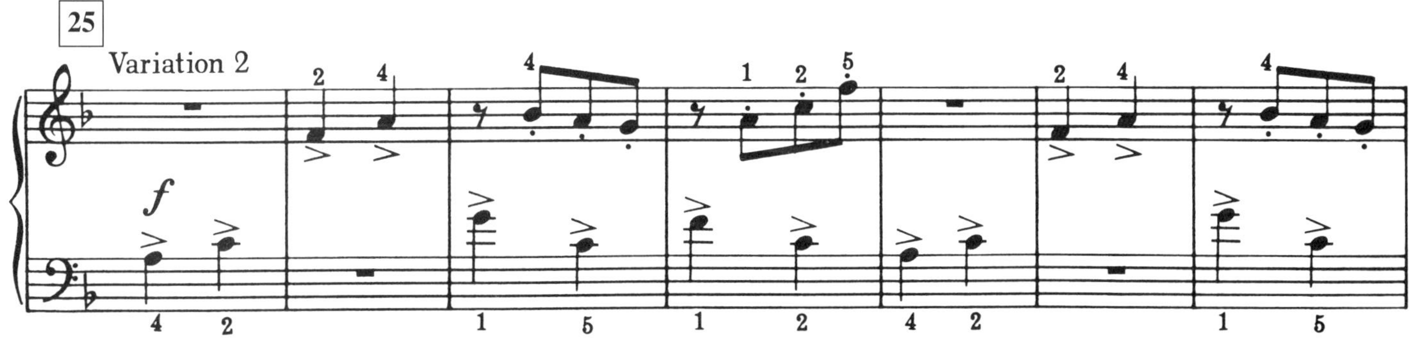
25
Variation 2
f

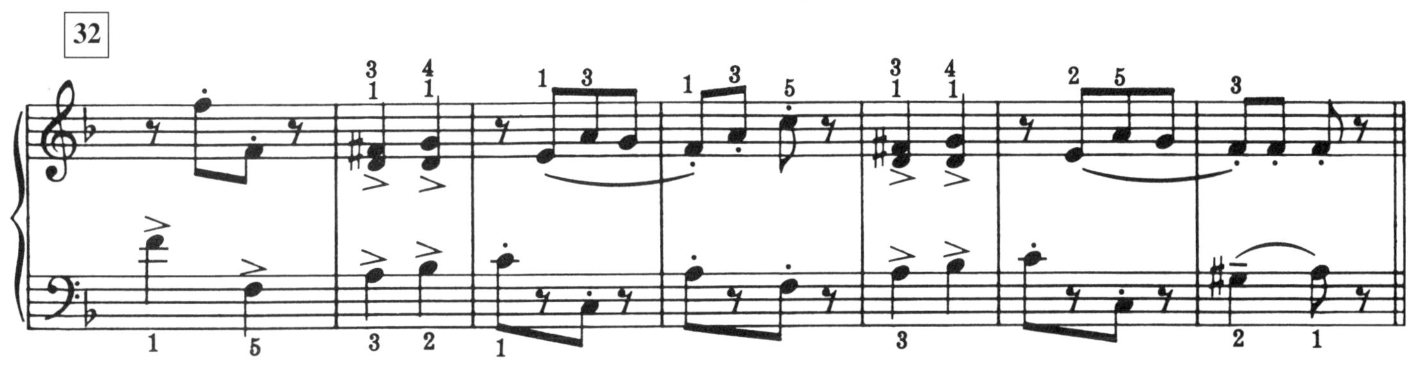
32

39
Variation 3
p
mf

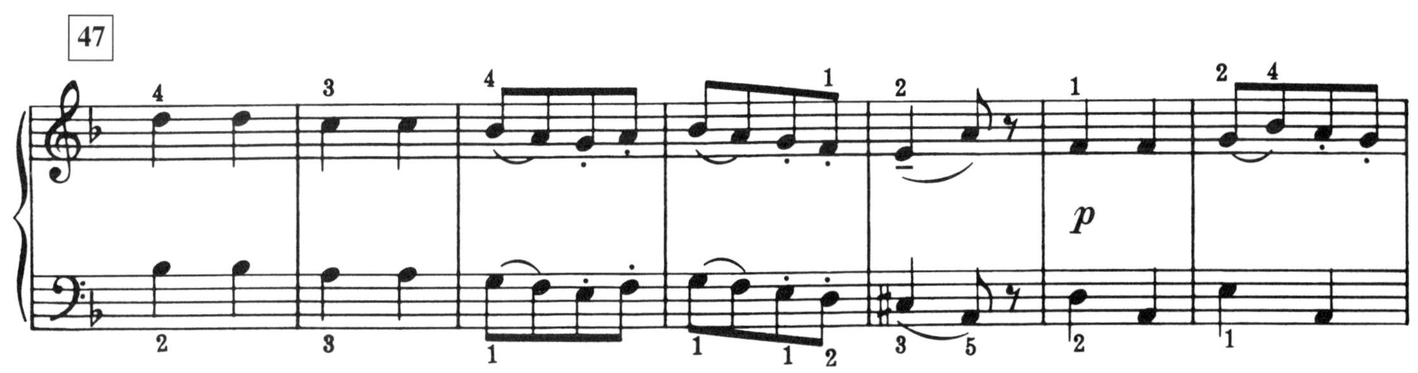
47
p

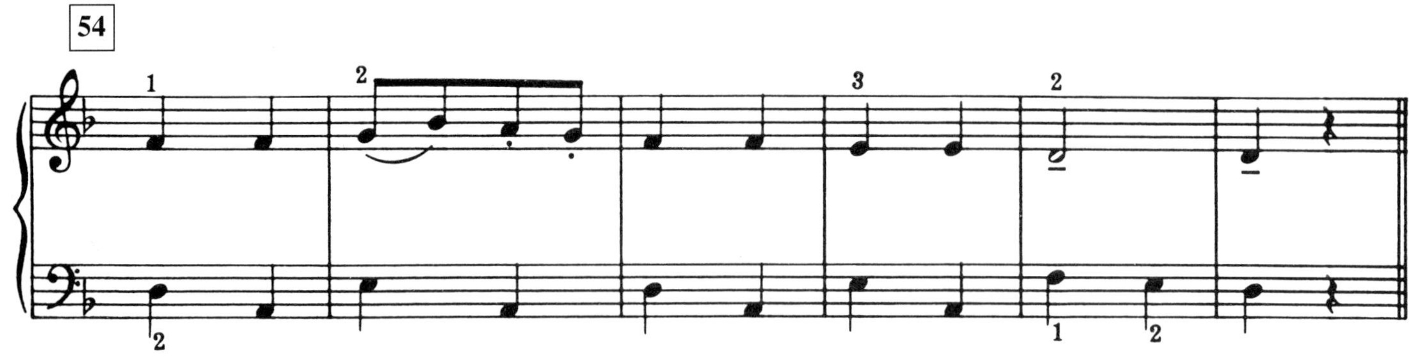
54

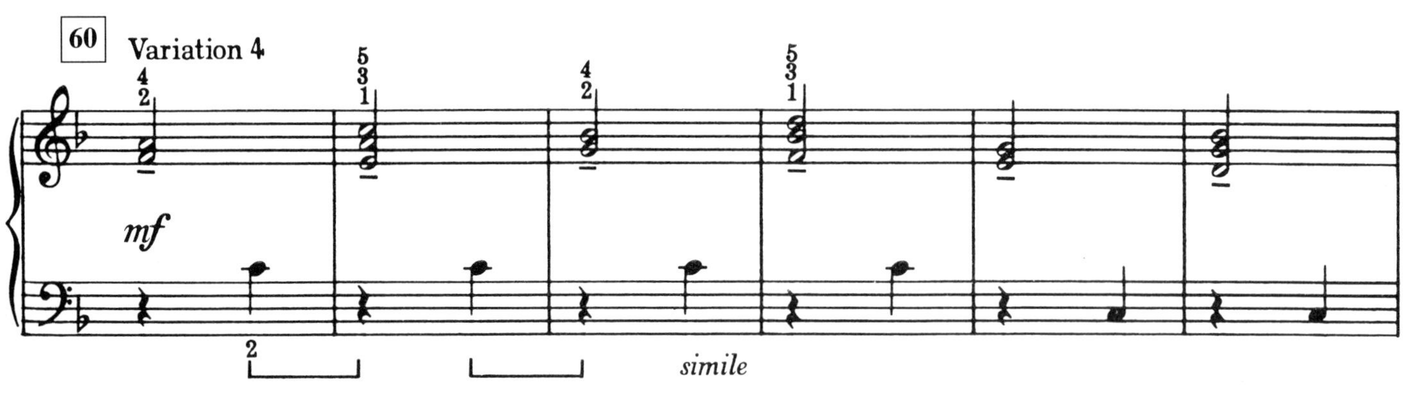
60
Variation 4
mf
simile

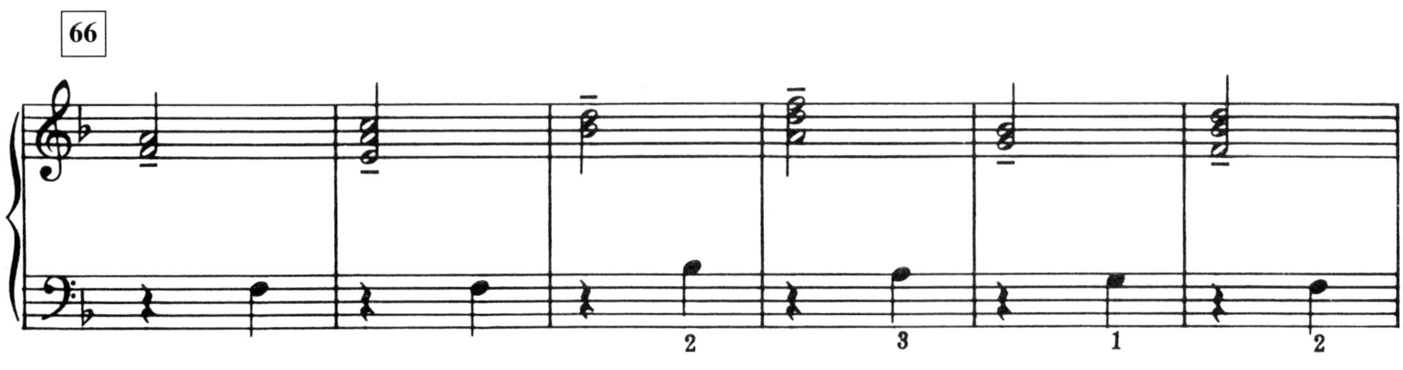
66

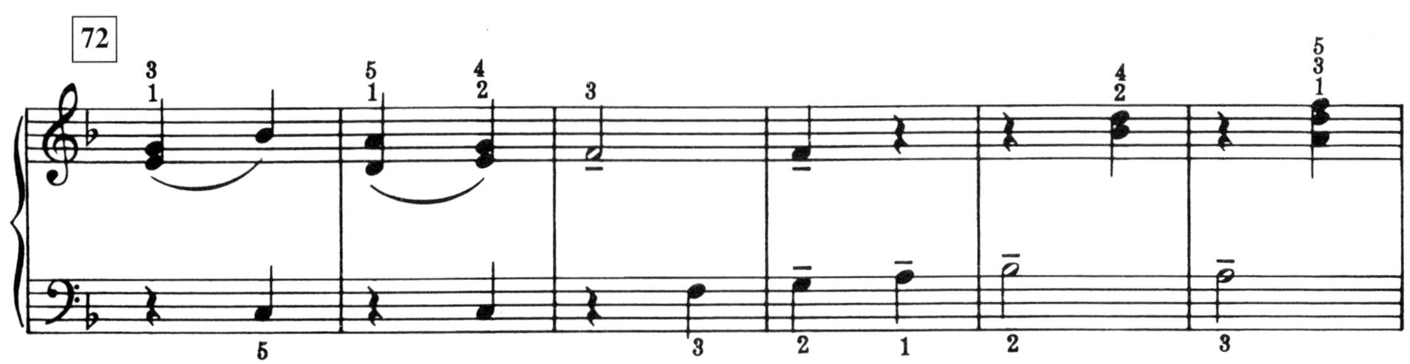
72

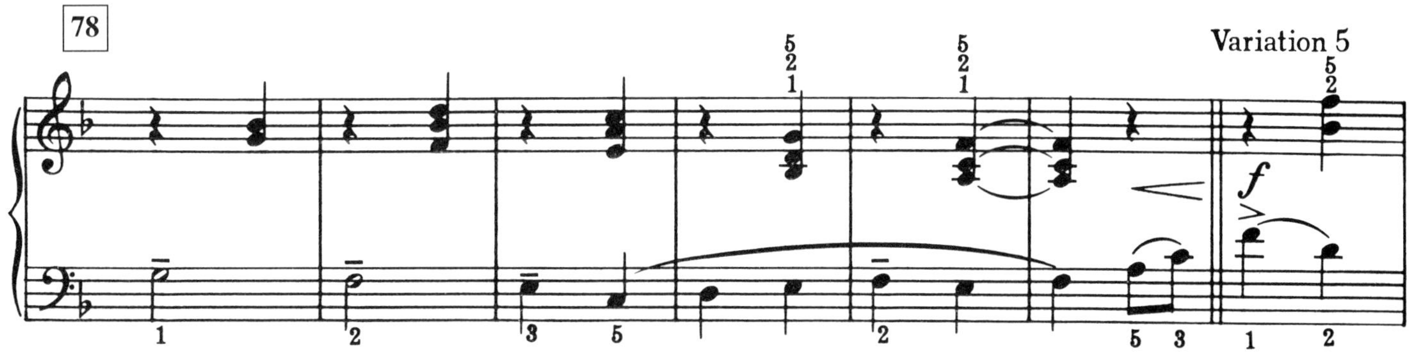
78
Variation 5
f

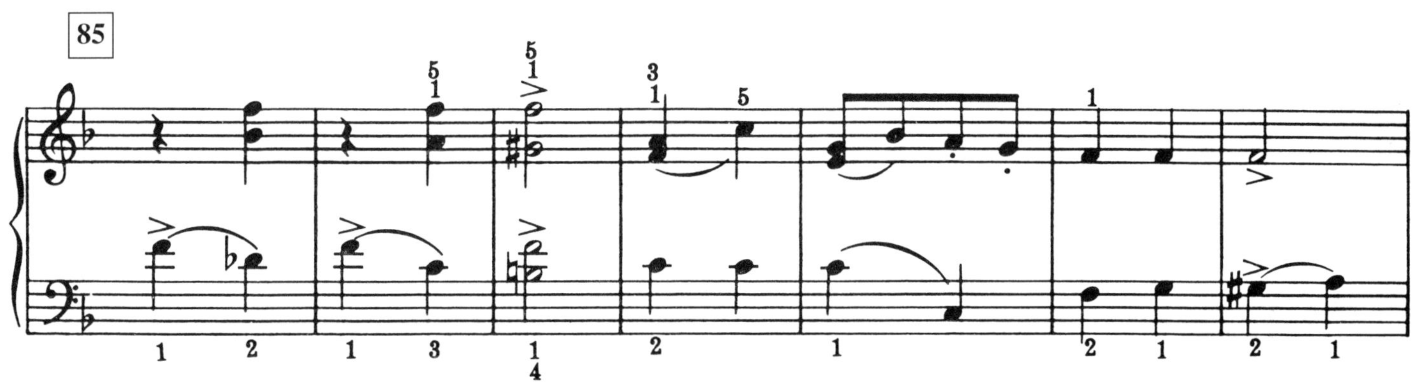
85

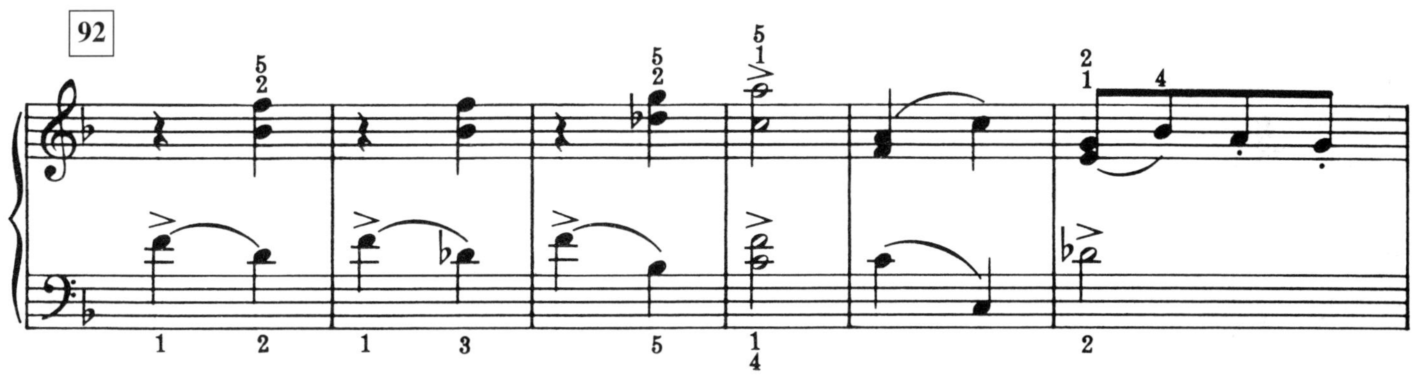
92

98
ff

Playing Soldiers

Rebikoff

Children's Song

Bartók

From "For Children" Book 1

Play Time

Bartók

From "For Children" Book 1

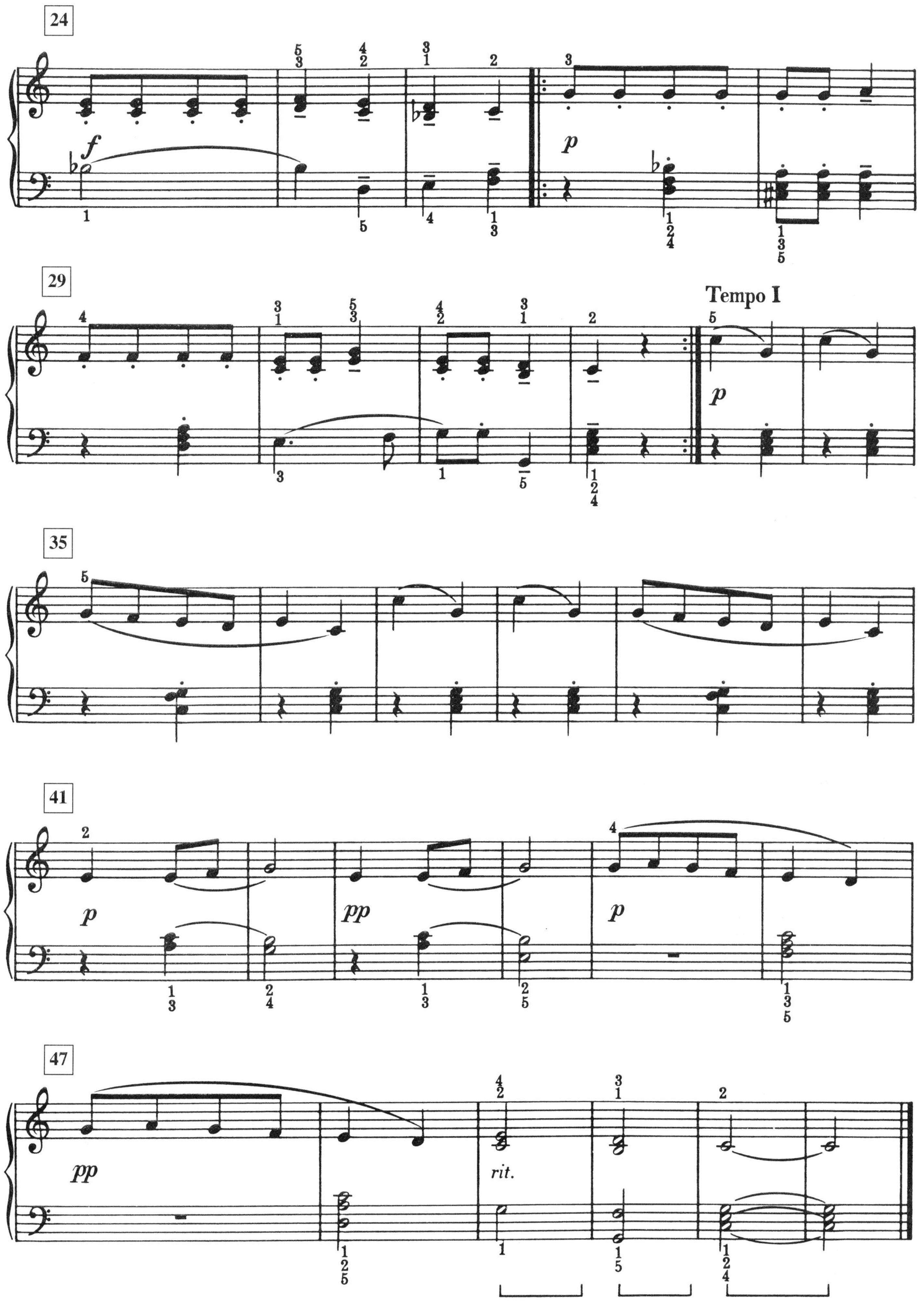
24
f
p
29
Tempo I
p
35
41
p
pp
p
47
pp
rit.

Hungarian Folk Song

Bartók

From "For Children" Book 1